SCIENCE IN
ANCIENT ROME

Other books by
Jacqueline L. Harris

Nine Black American Doctors
Martin Luther King, Jr.
Henry Ford

JACQUELINE L. HARRIS

SCIENCE IN ANCIENT ROME

A First Book
Franklin Watts   1988
New York   London   Toronto   Sydney

*Dedicated to my nephew, Timothy,
the historian in the family.*

Cover photograph by Photo Researchers, Inc. (Walter S. Clark)

Map by Vantage Art, Inc.

Photographs courtesy of: Art Resource: pp. 8, 19 (top), 40 (top),
46 (Alinari); The Bettmann Archive, Inc.: pp. 12, 16, 19 (bottom),
21, 25, 26 (bottom), 40 (bottom), 44, 49, 52, 59, 65; The Metropolitan
Museum of Art: pp. 26 (top), 30, 33

Library of Congress Cataloging-in-Publication Data

Harris, Jacqueline L.

Science in ancient Rome/Jacqueline L. Harris.
p.   cm.—(A First book)
Bibliography: p.
Includes index.
Summary: Describes how the Romans put to use and expanded the
scientific achievements of earlier civilizations.
ISBN 0-531-10595-4
1. Science—Rome—History—Juvenile literature. 2. Science,
Ancient—Juvenile literature. 3. Rome—Civilization—Juvenile
literature. [1. Science—Rome—History. 2. Science, Ancient.
3. Rome—Civilization.] I. Title.
Q127.R7H37   1988   88-2649
509.37—dc19   CIP   AC

CONTENTS

SCIENCE IN
ANCIENT ROME

Ruins of an Etruscan theater

1

THE PRACTICAL ROMANS: PUTTING SCIENCE TO WORK

The sky darkened over the Etruscan village of Veii in northern Italy. Soon the sky was filled with rolling, boiling clouds. Jagged streaks of lightning flickered from cloud to ground. Huddling in their grass-thatched homes, the Etruscans watched.

"Don't be afraid," said the wise old man of the village. "The lightning comes from the east—from the left hand of the god Tinia. It is a good sign."

The people smiled and sighed. Tinia, the king of the gods who lived in the northeastern skies, was pleased.

The year was 800 B.C. The Etruscan culture was the first civilization of any kind in what we know today as Italy. The Etruscans were the ancestors of those who conquered the Latins and turned a small river village into the city of Rome.

The Etruscan view that natural phenomena such as lightning was a message from the gods is very different from the way scientists think today. Scientists look at lightning and ask: "Why—what events of nature caused this to happen?" The Etruscans said, "It happened. What is the message?"

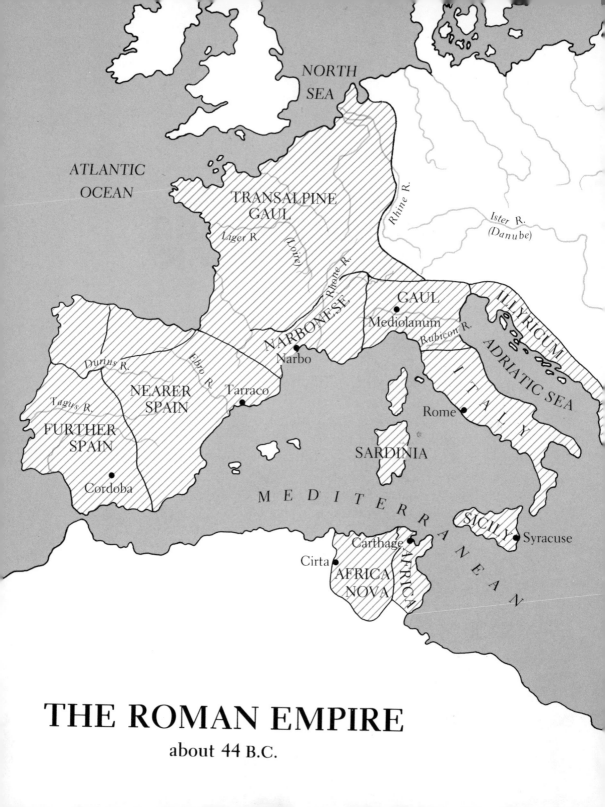

NORTH
SEA

ATLANTIC
OCEAN

TRANSALPINE
GAUL

Liger R.

(Loire)

Rhine R.

Ister R.
(Danube)

NARBONESE

Rhône R.

GAUL

Mediolanum

Rubicon R.

ILLYRICUM

Narbo

ADRIATIC SEA

I T A L Y

Durius R.

Ibro R.

NEARER
SPAIN

Tarraco

Rome

Tagus R.

FURTHER
SPAIN

SARDINIA

Cordoba

M E D I T E R R A N E A N

SICILY

Syracuse

Carthage

Cirta

AFRICA
NOVA

AFRICA

THE ROMAN EMPIRE
about 44 B.C.

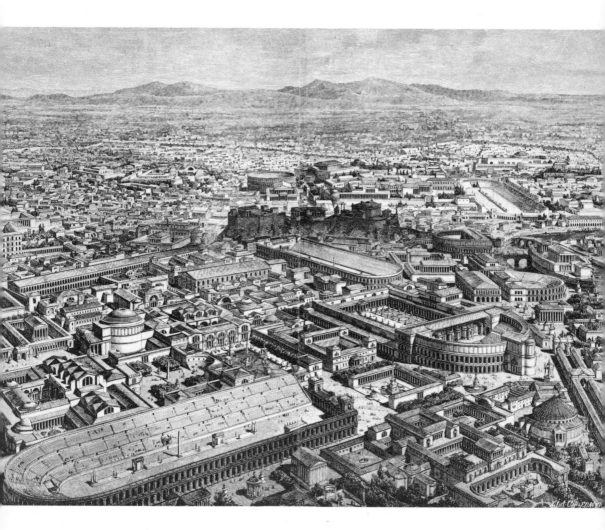

A reconstruction of the city of Rome, about the third
century A.D. *The domed building on the left is the
Pantheon (see Chapter 9); the round building in
the top center is the Colosseum (see Chapter 2).*

The word **science** is derived from the Latin word *scientia*, which means "knowledge." Scientific knowledge is obtained through observation—for example, observation of noise and flashes of light produced by thunder and lightning. Today we think of science as a search for truth. For the Romans, science was a collection of observations, the source of which they credited to the work of the gods. Their Etruscan heritage encouraged this way of thinking, which we might call superstition.

Other ancient peoples, the Greeks in particular, took the concept of science one step further—sorting out observations, classifying them, and developing certain theories or rules—sometimes testing their observations to see if they proved the theory. From this came certain truths that helped provide an understanding of the natural world. Seldom, if ever, did the Romans achieve this level of scientific activity. The Romans were largely content to accumulate the knowledge of others in books and writings and to give it practical application to benefit human life.

Although the Romans would make no contributions to basic science or scientific theory, they would make new and practical use of science. We call this applied science. The Romans would be the builders, the city planners, the engineers. They would perfect the use of metals, stone, and cement. Their accomplishments would leave an enduring mark on the horizons of Rome and most of the world.

The Romans were also great soldiers. By 146 B.C. all lands bordering on the Mediterranean were conquered and ruled by Rome. Rome became a wealthy world capital, the focus of Western civilization. The wealthy and the educated of many lands were drawn to Rome. Thus it was that the scientists of other countries traveled to Rome, and Rome benefited. The practical Romans took the scientific ideas being discussed in the city and put them to work.

In particular, Greek medical scientists came to Rome to tend to the illnesses of the important, wealthy people of Rome. Through their interest in what made people sick and what would make them well, a few Romans developed a more scientific point of view. Roman interest in medicine grew, and Romans made contributions to this discipline.

2

THE ROMAN BUILDERS: ARCHES AND CONCRETE

Monuments to the Roman builder can be seen throughout the city of Rome.

Rome's Ponte Milvio, a 2,400-year-old bridge that once rang to the clank of Roman legions on the march, now carries joggers, strollers, and bikers across the Tiber River.

Just down the street stands the Colosseum, an amphitheater built late in the first century A.D. as an arena for Roman games. One wall is broken away like the edge of an ice cream cone. Weeds invade the cobblestoned interior, unrivaled in size until 1914, when the Yale Bowl was built in New Haven, Connecticut. The Pantheon, the Roman temple to the gods and still the widest dome in the world, is an awesome sight to visitors.

Across the valleys and over the hills of Rome, you can see a trail of broken arches. Once that was the Aqua Claudia, an aqueduct that carried fresh spring water to the residents of Rome. On the outskirts of Rome, the Appian Way is still visible—abandoned now for the expressways but once a main highway in an 180,000-mile (290,000-km) system, helping to extend Rome's influence and power north into Britain and south to North Africa.

Ruins of the Colosseum

These arched spans, these immense buildings, these enduring roads tell the remarkable story of the Roman engineers. Using simple tools and muscle power, they took the ideas of others and put them to work serving the people's needs.

THE ARCH

What was the secret of the Roman engineers' monumental achievement? One answer was their recognition of the possibilities of the arch.

The arch may appear to be simply a beautiful, elegant decoration. But the arch also has the kind of strength needed to span long distances and enclose larger areas. Today large steel girders—something not available to Roman engineers—provide that kind of strength.

The arch was conceived by the Egyptians and Greeks. They discovered that wedge-shaped stones formed into an arch exerted two opposing sets of forces that cancel each other out. Thus, the stones support one another. The Etruscans and later the Romans used this half-circle shape to provide support over doors and windows. They found the arch stronger than a straight support. But only when the Romans began to develop and improve the arch was its true strength discovered. Roman engineers found that, properly designed, the arch could form the main support for bridges. A series of arches could support enormous domed ceilings for majestic buildings.

SUPERSTRONG CONCRETE

In the third century the Romans discovered a way to make a very strong concrete, a material invented by the Egyptians. **Concrete** is a mixture of powdered lime and water to which sand and stone are added. Near the volcano Vesuvius, in southwest Italy, the Romans found a large deposit of sandlike volcanic ash that, when added to lime paste, formed a concrete as hard as natural rock.

Now the Roman builders had a design and a strong material that would enable them to become master engineers. A series of arches built in a riverbed formed the foundation of a bridge. The arches were held up by large, square, upright supports (piers) built into the riverbed. The engineers found that too many large piers obstructed the flow of the water. When water flow is obstructed, its force is increased. This rushing water scours sand and gravel from the river bottom, weakening the pier's attachment to the bottom. To solve this problem, the Romans used larger arches. There were fewer piers in the river, and the force of the river water was not destructively high.

Many of the Roman bridges constructed over main rivers were huge and still stand today. In Spain, near the border with Portugal, the Lacers Bridge extends 600 feet (180 m) across the Tagus River at a height of 175 feet (53 m). Another Spanish bridge, crossing the Guadiana River, is an amazing 2,500 feet (760 m) long.

BUILDING
A WATER SYSTEM

Adapting the idea of bridges to land construction, the Romans built huge **aqueducts**—concrete-walled channels supported by tall arches. The aqueducts carried spring water to Rome from streams in the Apennine Mountains 15 miles (24 km) east of the city. As the Roman Empire expanded, Roman engineers built aqueducts to serve cities in Spain, North Africa, and Greece.

A system very much like water distribution systems in use

Above: *a Roman bridge in Spain*
Below: *a Roman aqueduct in Spain*

today transported the water from the aqueduct to various parts of the city. Surging in from the mountains, the water flowed into holding tanks, where sand and rocks were allowed to settle out. From there the water was distributed through lead or clay pipes to the fountains, baths, factories, and homes. Only important people could have water piped into their houses. For them a simple turning of a bronze faucet supplied a drink of water.

ARCHED ROOFS AND DOMES

The Romans found other uses for the arch in magnificent buildings. They discovered that constructing long, thick concrete arches produced a shape like half a barrel. This **barrel vault** was used to roof large public buildings. Now huge supporting timbers cluttering the insides of buildings were no longer needed. Crossing two long, thick arches at right angles produced a large, square-roofed building. These crossed arches were called groined or **cross vaults.** Adapting the arch idea—using wedge-shaped stones to form a self-supporting half-circle shape—they produced domed roofs.

Arches and domes require thick supporting walls. The Romans found that a kind of corrugated wall with thick sections at regular intervals provided good support. These thick parts are called buttresses.

As they built their arches and domes, a new and beautiful city emerged from amid the square-roofed and raftered buildings. Other major building projects produced coliseums, sewer systems, and public bathhouses.

BUILDING
A HIGHWAY SYSTEM

The excellent Roman highway system was built mainly to enable the army to move quickly. Roman roads were sometimes called

The Appian Way,
the famous Roman road

"walls lying on their sides" because they were so well built. The roads, made of four or five layers of sand, gravel, cement, and stone, were usually at least 4 feet (1.2 m) thick—four times as thick as our modern highways—and anywhere from 6 to 20 feet (2 to 6 m) wide. To serve travelers, maps, inns, and other conveniences were provided at way stations along the roads. Among those using the roads was the official government postal service.

Roman builders changed the horizon of many a city, filling the edges that met the sky with soaring domes and graceful arches. Their engineering genius eased the traveler's journey with a bridge or a paved road.

3

THE ROMAN ARCHITECTS: BUILDING HOMES

Rome began as a small river village of straw huts lining narrow alleys in 753 B.C. By 300 B.C., graceful, columned public buildings with arched, domed ceilings were rising amid the straw huts. Imaginative Roman architects were providing Romans with a modern-day choice of home design—apartments, homes, and mansions. Some designs offered such conveniences as running water and a sewage waste disposal system.

The earliest Roman homes consisted of a series of rooms built in the shape of an O. In the center of the O was an open courtyard. Beneath the open roof a deep cistern, or collecting well, stored rainwater for the family's use. The courtyard was the cooking area. This courtyard, its walls blackened with cooking fire smoke, came to be known as the atrium, from *ater*, the Latin word for "black." This design was improved upon by decorating the courtyard with columns and flower gardens.

VILLAS FOR SOME

For some prosperous Romans, architects designed country houses, or **villas.** The villa had a main building with two wings—a bedroom wing and a bath wing, supplied with aqueduct water. The bath wing resembled what today would be an indoor swimming pool. Along the back of the villa, the owner could enjoy the view and the gardens from a covered walkway lined with stone columns.

APARTMENTS FOR OTHERS

Architects also built five-story apartment houses, called **insulae**. *Insulae* were built of brick and sometimes took up a whole block. Depending on the money available, the apartment dweller could rent a small, dark single room or a luxurious two-floor apartment. Since there were no elevators, it was better to live on the lower floors. The lower floors were also closer to the running water supplied by the aqueduct system. *Insulae* dwellers had their own toilets in the basement of the building. Other city dwellers had to use the public toilets.

In the earliest homes, wooden shutters were used to cover windows. The Romans invented glass windowpanes, and the room with a view became a feature of Roman homes. Glass was also used to build greenhouses, which collected sunlight. These were favorite places for putting solar energy to work in the winter to grow cucumbers, a popular snack food.

A SECURITY SYSTEM

Roman builders put locks, a Roman invention, on many of the homes they built. The Roman lock, a more advanced adaptation of a kind of Egyptian latch, was similar in design to the kind we use today. This is how it worked.

The bolt had several holes in it. The lock was fitted with pins in the same pattern as the holes in the bolt. When the lock was brought into position over the bolt, the pins dropped into the

Ruins of a house at Pompeii

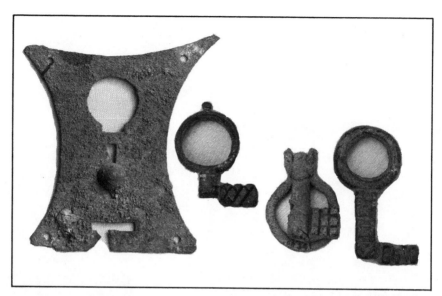

TEPIDARIVM   CONCAMERATA SVDATIO   BALNEVM

TEPIDA
BALN

CALI
DA

LACONICVM   LABRVM

HYPO   CAVS   TVM

matching holes, and the bolt was locked. To unlock the bolt, a key with prongs was used to push the pins up out of the bolt.

Many Roman homes also had central heating, thanks to the inventiveness of Sergius Orata, a Roman fish merchant. He decided to try to find a way to raise fish and oysters in the winter for sale in his fish market.

Orata built special fish tanks raised on brick posts with small fire pits to the side. The fire kept the water just warm enough so that the fish flourished. From this Orata got the idea for building villas with heated bath wings. Heat from an underground furnace circulated through ducts under the bath floor. This invention led to the development of a way to heat whole houses during winter. This system was called a **hypocaustum**, from the Latin words for "under" and "burn."

The *hypocaustum* system brought about a change in the basic style of the Roman house. The atrium was eliminated, and the house was built in a solid block because that design was easier to heat.

Many other items invented or improved by the Romans made homes more comfortable—like staircases, soap, wax candles, bedsprings, and curtains. As a result, the convenience and comfort of many Roman homes were similar to that which we enjoy today.

Above: *lock plate (top) and keys.* Below: *a drawing of a Roman bathhouse showing the heating system. On the right is the tub; on the left is the steam room.*

4

THE ROMAN MINERS: BRASS AND GOLD

It is 3000 B.C. Fire, ash, and huge red-hot rocks explode through a cone-shaped opening in the earth's crust. A volcano, set off by the shifting of rocky layers deep inside the earth, has erupted. Rivers of melted rock flow down the sides of the volcano. Cooling, they settle on the lower slopes and valleys, layering the land with a metal-rich rocky layer.

A STRANGE, RUSTY ROCK

Hundreds of years later, someone tosses a few bright blue rocks into a charcoal fire. The rocks soon glow hot and later cool into hard, rust-colored rocks. Someone hammers the strange rock with another rock and finds that it doesn't break. Instead, it changes its shape. Yielding to the blows, the strange rock is made into something useful—a knife, a sickle.

The rock was copper, probably one of the first minerals to be mined. Once early miners had discovered the value of the blue rock, they began to search for it. They found many outcroppings—places where the copper ore emerged from the surface of the land.

It was a simple matter to dig up the ore with crude shovels and picks. When outcroppings ran out, the miners dug into the earth.

ETRUSCAN MINERS DIG IN

The Colline Metallifere ("Metalliferous Hills") in northern Italy were rich in the metals iron, zinc, tin, and copper. And the Etruscans who settled in the area in 900 B.C. were the first in Italy to see the value of these metals. They used the mining methods of the day.

Digging trenches was one such way to mine. When surface deposits ran out, the miners dug deeper. First they dug a series of pits 50 feet (15 m) deep. Then they connected the bottoms of the pits with horizontal tunnels. Next the miners descended through the pits into the tunnels and dug the ore from the walls of the tunnels.

ROMAN GOLD MINES

Roman miners had only the simplest tools—iron picks, spades, and hammers and wedges (prying tools) made of deer horns. Copper ore was especially hard and often difficult to dig out with these tools. Copper miners often turned to their tried-and-true tool—fire—to solve this problem. They built a fire against the rocky ore bed. When the ore was very hot, they threw water against it, shattering the rock.

Gold, because it was rare, was a very valuable metal. Roman miners developed a special method for gold mining. First they dug tunnels beneath a mountain until the mountain collapsed. Then they diverted a large mountain stream through a channel across the caved-in mountain. The bottom of the channel had been

Gold and silver jewelry

planted with a small plant called gorse, which trapped the gold as the water rushed past.

SOLVING THE
FLOODING PROBLEM

The water that seeped into mine trenches or pits from rainfall and surrounding rock layers was a serious problem for the miners. Bucket brigades—people standing in line passing buckets of water along—were used to bail out the mines. Pliny, a Roman writer, describes one bucket brigade 1,500 feet (460 m) long, bringing up water from the mine day and night.

Later the Romans used mechanical devices to pump water from their mines. One device was the waterwheel, carrying huge buckets of water up from the mine, pouring out the water at the top, and descending for another load of water. The waterwheel was powered by people walking a treadmill at the hub. A treadmill is a device that one or more persons walks on, their steps turning a wheel.

Another device, called Archimedes' screw, a kind of giant corkscrew, was used to force water up an incline. This too was powered by a treadmill.

Work in the mines was hard and miserable. Most of the miners were slaves. They worked day and night, never seeing the sun, breathing dusty air, carrying rocks that weighed as much as 100 pounds (45 kg). Some worked every day, constantly walking the treadmills.

REFINING THE METAL

Once the ore was mined, it had to be sorted, crushed, and washed. Often the metal was combined with impurities, which made the metal less useful. Smelting, or purifying, copper ore was done in fire pits dug into the earth. The pits were lined with clay. A wood fire was started in the pit, then layers of wood and ore were added. Clay was used to cover the pit.

Refined or purified iron did not prove to be a strong and useful metal. Iron swords bent at the first twang against a foe's sword. But many experimental steps finally produced a way to use iron to make a strong metal called steel. In a method called cementation, red-hot iron was hammered over a charcoal fire, causing the charcoal fumes to combine with the iron. Then the hot metal was quenched, or plunged into cold water.

STEEL—A SECRET WEAPON

Although the Romans are not credited with developing iron into steel, which is stronger, they were the first to put steel to use. The steel sword became Rome's secret weapon, earning for its legions the conquest of most of the known world.

It is interesting to note that not everyone agreed on how iron should be used. Pliny wrote: "Iron is the most precious and at the same time the worst metal for mankind. By its help we cleave the earth, establish tree nurseries, fell trees, . . . build houses, hew stone . . . but this metal serves also for war, murder and robbery . . . and this I hold to be the most blameworthy product of the human mind."

OTHER
METALWORKING IDEAS

Like iron, pure copper is not a sturdy metal, but someone discovered that making it into an **alloy**—that is, mixing it with other metals—produced a very strong metal.

The Romans excelled at making metal alloys and in so doing displayed a basic talent for experimental chemistry, for testing and

Silver spoons and bowls

retesting to learn the proper formula to use. They are credited with producing **brass** by mixing just the right amounts of copper and zinc ore. The two ores were then heated over a charcoal fire. The charcoal changed the zinc ore to zinc vapor, which combined with the copper. Sturdy as **bronze** (another copper alloy), brass was easier to work and more attractive. It was used to make coins, decorative tableware such as cups and plates, and dress armor and helmets.

Roman metalworkers also discovered a modern way to purify gold ore. They crushed the ore and mixed it with mercury. The gold dissolved out of the ore and into the mercury. They then poured the mercury through a leather filter. The filtered mercury was heated. When the mercury was completely boiled off, the gold remained.

Other, similar processes used to produce pure gold and silver further demonstrate that the Romans had a good grasp of a chemical technique still in use today. That technique uses the dissolving power of substances to remove impurities.

Gold and silver, precious because they were rare, were used to buy goods and to make jewelry and decorative items. Roman dentists also used gold to make supports for false teeth.

5

THE ROMAN FARMERS: WHEAT AND GRAPES

When the first farmers set foot on the land near Rome, they found a forest of beech, oak, laurel, and pine. The trees were the first major plants to take hold on a land formed by layer upon layer of ash from volcanic eruptions. Settling beneath the trees, decaying leaves and plants were forming a rich topsoil. Given perhaps another two thousand years, a thick layer of soil rich with the minerals and foods needed to grow crops would have been produced.

But to the first settlers, the trees were fuel and building material. And they wanted the land for growing crops and building settlements. At first, their crude stone axes were no match for the trees. But they were clever and strong; they made larger, sharper stone axes and began the deforestation of what is now western Italy.

By 700 B.C., the Etruscans were using metal axes. The land clearing speeded up. The thin soil, what there was of it, was rich.

ANCIENT ROMAN
FARMING

The first Roman farmers, using crude wooden plows, scratched small furrows in the earth and planted seed. The rich topsoil yielded a good crop of rye or wheat for perhaps two growing seasons. When the soil gave out, the farmer moved on to a new plot.

As the Roman farmers struggled to grow food in the thin layers of topsoil, they devised many new ways to feed their crops.

It seemed important to make sure the plants could get all of the food in the soil. They devised a plowing method that produced crumbly, almost dustlike soil. This was done by repeated plowing of the field—plowing, then cross-plowing, then plowing again. Then the seed was plowed into the soil.

An observation that fields where cattle and sheep had grazed seemed more fertile probably led to a major development for Roman farmers—fertilizer. The animal manure had enriched the fields. The Roman farmer sought animals—cows, sheep, horses— whose manure was especially good for crops. Those farmers who did not have animals built compost pits. Into this pit went household garbage, dead plants, leaves, straw, ashes, and available animal manure. Pigeon and chicken manure was found to be especially rich. Soil was also added to the pit. An oak stake was driven into the center and used to stir the compost from time to time. This compost was used to fertilize the farmer's fields.

Another Roman fertilization method was planting certain plants that were known to enrich the soil—beans, clover, and alfalfa. The Romans probably discovered that when fields of such wild plants were plowed up before planting, the soil was unusually fertile. Today we know that these plants are nitrogen-fixing plants; that is, these plants remove the important plant food, nitrogen, from the air and add it to the soil. These nitrogen-fixing plants were plowed into the soil, a process called green manuring.

ROTATING CROPS

Another Roman farming technique, probably adapted from their earlier custom of moving from plot to plot, was crop rotation. A field planted with wheat was next planted with rye or oats. Then a nitrogen-fixing crop would be planted. This gave the soil a chance to recover the foods used by different crops. Sometimes Roman farmers would let a field lie idle, or fallow, every other year. But only if they planted nitrogen-fixing plants or added fertilizer did this help the next crop grow.

Roman farmers knew that they had to keep their fields carefully drained or their farms would turn into swamps. They cut drainage ditches across their land, filling them with stones or branches.

Their ideas about fertilizer and drainage led to abundant harvests of wheat, rye, oats, and barley. Made healthy by the good grain supply, the Roman population grew. But gradually, the thin topsoil was running out. The removal of hillside trees for lumber accelerated the loss of topsoil. Rainwater normally trapped in the hillside forestland ran down the hills, washing topsoil into the rivers and streams and creating swamps in the valleys.

The farmers tried to stop the erosion with drains, dikes, and dams. But with their limited tools they made little impact on the large erosion problem.

FAMINE STRIKES

Erosion, worn-out topsoil, and swampy fields caused many farmers to abandon their land. The supply of grain decreased, and many Romans went to bed hungry day after day. In the mid-fourth century B.C., famine struck the city. The government bought grain from other countries. But it was not enough. In the year 436 B.C., the famine was so severe that thousands of starving people threw themselves into the Tiber River.

There was only one solution. Rome needed more land—more good grainfields. The Roman army marched, conquering Tuscany, the land of the Etruscans, and taking Sicily and its rich wheatlands away from the Carthaginians. The grain supply problem was solved for the time being.

WAR DESTROYS FARMLAND

But picking a fight with Carthage, a powerful city-state on the coast of what is now North Africa, set off the Punic Wars, a series of wars over the next hundred years that Rome eventually won. But for Rome's farmland the price was a terrible one. For more than twelve straight years in the latter part of the second century B.C., battles raged back and forth across the villages and fields of Rome's farm belt. Usually, the victor burned the grainfields and crops and chased off the cattle and farmers.

When the wars were finally over, Rome found itself with 2 million acres (800,000 ha) of ruined land whose owners had died in battle or fled for their lives. The government offered the land for sale or lease. Only the rich could afford the price or provide the labor and materials needed to work the devastated land. Roman farmland became huge estates of the rich. And growing grain to feed hungry Romans was no longer necessary, since Rome could import grain from its conquered lands.

NEW CROPS—
GRAPES AND OLIVES

Wealthy Roman farmers turned to two plants that were found growing in Greece—grapes and olives. These are called cash crops because they can be used to make valuable products. Grapes can be made into wine, and olives can be made into oil.

Grapevines are started from cuttings from growing vines. By simply taking cuttings from successful grapevines, farmers can make sure they grow only plants that produce a good harvest. The Roman farmer perfected this technique and is credited with producing the first grapevines to flourish in an ocean climate. Grapevines do not generally do well in high-salt soils.

MAKING WINE

Most of the grape harvest was used to make wine. The grapes were crushed and the juice poured into huge 100-gallon (400-liter) jars. After about a week, when the grape juice had fermented into wine, the jars were sealed and buried in moist sand or in cool cellars.

Good wines must have just the proper balance of sweetness and sourness. The flavor of the grapes is the key to good wine. Roman farmers found that a sunny hillside was the best place to grow sweet grapes; cooler areas produced tangy grapes. They learned that soil on volcanic slopes, of which there were many in Italy, produced grapes with excellent flavors.

By the first century A.D., Roman wines were known throughout the world for their flavor. And to this day Italy is known for its wines.

Romans spread their grape-growing talent to other parts of their empire. They created the famous Bordeaux vineyards in what is now southwestern France. They established vineyards in France's Loire River valley, where the grapes are used to make some of the most famous white wines. Romans also introduced vineyards to the Rhine River valley in what is now southwestern Germany, an area famous for its tangy, sweet Rhine wines.

GROWING OLIVES

Sinking deep roots into moisture-laden soil layers, olive trees were well suited to the dry soil near Rome. Like grapes, olive trees are started from cuttings. The Roman farmers found their skill in the

vineyard useful in the development of olive trees. The trees thrived in the sunny Roman climate and produced abundant crops of olives.

Olives were an important food and also prized for their oil, which was used for cooking and as a lamp fuel. The oil was made by crushing the olives between two large round stones.

As the Romans extended their control into semidesert North African areas in what is now Algeria, Tunisia, and Lebanon, they brought their ideas about agriculture. Olive trees were particularly successful in these areas and brought a prosperity to North Africa that lasted for many centuries. The introduction of an important cash crop, olive trees, to North Africa is perhaps Rome's most important contribution to agriculture.

Above: *hauling and carrying grapes.* Below: *jars for storing wine, oil, and grain*

6

THE ROMAN PHYSICIANS: HELPING THE SICK

"Drink cabbage juice."

"Eat goat fat."

This medical advice was about all there was for the sick of ancient Rome in the second century B.C.

Meanwhile, in Greece, medicine was taking its first fumbling steps as a science. As the Roman legions swept south, conquering Greece in the third century B.C., Romans came in contact with Greek medicine. Greek medicine sought the cause of disease, or sickness, and ways to cure it. Such ideas were a threat to the Roman way of life, one in which illness was accepted as the will of the gods. Marcus Cato, a Roman general and leader, who was opposed to the influence of Greece, wrote: "Whenever that nation [Greece] shall bestow its literature upon us, it will corrupt everything and all the sooner if it sends its physicians here. They have conspired among themselves to murder all foreigners with their medicine."

GREEK PHYSICIANS
COME TO ROME

But some ill Romans disagreed with Cato's view; Greek physicians, or medical doctors, often found themselves sought by the sick of Rome. Thus began what has been called Hellenistic medicine—Greek-trained physicians attracted to Rome, the world center of wealth and power.

Archagathos was one of the first Greek physicians to practice in Rome. He quickly became famous as a healer of wounds. In gratitude, Rome granted him citizenship. But his reckless cruelty in cutting soon earned for him a new kind of fame. He became known as the Carnifex, the butcher.

Asclepiades (as kluh PE uh deez) came to Rome in 100 B.C. as a teacher and public speaker. One day, while speaking to a street gathering, he saw a funeral passing by. Something about the body made him think that the person was not really dead. Sure enough, a little massage and cold water proved Asclepiades correct. His fame as a physician who could achieve remarkable cures quickly spread.

As he worked as a physician, Asclepiades developed a theory of illness based on the concept that the body was made up of tiny particles. When these particles were not properly arranged, the person got sick. The problem for the sick person was to get the particles back in order. To accomplish this, Asclepiades advised sunshine, massage, exercise, warmth, cold baths, drinking liquids, and special diets.

HEALING THE SICK

Asclepiades was the first to perceive the difference between acute mental diseases—diseases of the mind that lasted a short time—and chronic mental diseases, those that lasted a long time. He

43

pioneered treatment for the mentally ill that is still used today. He calmed his patients with herbs, music, sunshine, and gentleness. He found that many of his patients could not pay attention or remember things. He devised exercises to help them with these problems. This was far different from the cruel treatment many mentally ill received in Rome, where the only treatment was to keep them in dark cellars.

With the successes of Asclepiades, the idea that something could be done about disease was taking hold in Rome.

Surgeons were encouraged to develop their skills in operating on people. They learned to tie off blood vessels to reduce bleeding during surgery. In the past a good surgeon had been one who could work steadily and carefully despite the cries of pain of the patient. But surgeons learned that the juices of certain plants could dull the pain. Two hundred different surgical instruments, or tools, were developed. Surgeons began to cure by cutting off badly mangled limbs, setting broken bones, removing tonsils, and taking out tumors, or growths.

CURING THE BLIND

Surgeons were especially successful in treating cataracts, a condition that clouds the lens of the eye, producing blindness. Roman surgeons learned that they could use a needle to gently tease the cloudy outer covering of the eye away from the eyeball. Once this outer coating was removed, the person could see better.

As the Roman patients presented their complaints of aches, lumps, and fevers, the doctors often faced hundreds of questions

Above: *Asclepiades*
treating a patient's arm
Below: *surgical tools*

for which there were no answers. But doctors like Rufus, a Greek from Ephesus, provided some of the answers. He discovered how the heart moves blood through the arteries, major blood vessels that carry the blood away from the heart. He found out how to tell which nerves move muscles and which ones give us the sense of touch. He discovered that fever is a part of the body's effort to kill disease organisms.

A doctor needing to know what disease his patient had could turn to the writings of Aretaeus (are uh TEE us). This physician studied and described the symptoms of diseases that affected the lungs, the nerves, the liver, the heart, and the brain. He was the first to describe diabetes, a disease produced when the body fails to use sugar properly.

Soranus' writings provided advice about delivering babies and caring for them after birth. He devised special instruments to use to deliver babies.

WHAT CAUSES DISEASES?

Asclepiades had won Roman acceptance of the idea that something could be done to cure disease. And physicians like Rufus and Aretaeus provided knowledge about the body and disease. But they worked amid a growing disagreement about what caused disease. To know this was to devise ways to cure it.

Into this atmosphere came Galen, whose parents were Greek and who was well trained in Greek science and medicine. He was determined to introduce science into medicine. His supreme self-confidence seemed to offer the answer to all questions. "I alone have indicated the true methods of treating diseases," he wrote.

He had a talent for diagnosis (determining what is wrong with sick people) and for treatment, talents that quickly came to the attention of the important people of Rome. He cured the illness of the wife of an important official. He identified the reason a famous philosopher could not move three of his fingers.

GALEN—THE
MEDICAL LEADER

Quickly, Galen became the medical genius of Rome. Emperors and senators called him to their sickbeds. His medical lectures drew crowds of educated and important Romans. With his skill, his influence, and his self-confidence, Galen became the natural leader of Roman physicians.

Galen wrote five hundred medical books, detailing his studies and his theories about disease and treatment. One important book, *The Uses of the Parts of the Body of Man*, described his studies of anatomy and physiology, how the body is made and how it works. Some of his more important studies of the function of the heart, the brain, the nerves, and the kidneys are described. He showed that nerves controlled breathing and that urine was produced by the kidneys. He described experiments on animals that proved for the first time that the heart pumped blood through the arteries. This book, which described studies on living animals, has earned for Galen the credit for founding experimental physiology.

GALEN'S BOOK
ON DISEASE

Another important Galen work was *On Parts Affected by Disease*, an organ-by-organ description of disease. But Galen followed up his descriptions of diseases with a theory that a person's personality causes certain diseases, a theory of the Greek physician Hippocrates. Galen had mixed sound scientific observation with an old and basically nonscientific idea. This and other errors, such as the idea

Galen

that pus formation was a normal part of the body's efforts to heal wounds, remained unquestioned by physicians for many centuries. Although the acceptance of these errors is a tribute to Galen's influence and stature as a physician in Rome, it held back the progress of medicine for many decades.

ROMAN MEDICINE DIES

When Galen died in 200 A.D., Rome lost its medical leader. Without the stimulus of Galen's lectures and writings, Rome gradually abandoned the experimental approach to medicine. Rome returned to religion and magic for cures, to camel's brain and turtle's blood for seizures, or fits, to sacrifices to Scabies, goddess of the itch, and to Febris, goddess of fever.

During Galen's lifetime Romans came the closest to understanding and participating in medical science as we understand it today, a search for the why and how of a phenomenon.

7

PUBLIC HEALTH IN ROME: SEWERS AND AQUEDUCTS

Bad air. The stench of swampy air frequently drifted over the hills of ancient Rome from the swampy valleys below. It was worrisome to many, for they knew that bad air, "mal aria" (in Latin, *male* means "bad" and *aer* means "air"), caused the shaking and feverish sickness that came to be known as **malaria**. Today we know that marshy areas are indeed a source of malaria. They are breeding grounds for the kind of mosquito that spreads the disease with its bite.

The "bad air" of Rome was a community problem, and combating it called for the joint effort of all Romans.

Launching a community effort to protect the public health is something we take for granted today. But in those days it was a new idea. Ancient Rome is justly famous for its impressive efforts to protect the health of its citizens. Its efforts are all the more impressive when you realize how little was known at the time about contagious diseases and how they are passed from person to person.

DRAINING THE SWAMPS

One of the first engineering tasks undertaken by Roman engineers was to dig trenches in the swamps to drain the marshy valleys. The work began in 500 B.C. under Tarquin the Proud, the last Etruscan king of Rome.

Driven by their talent for organization and engineering, the Romans built sewage systems not only in Rome but also in all of the major cities of their empire.

The first sewer was actually the trenching dug to drain the marshes. Lined with stone, the trench was designed to carry off rainwater. As the years passed, the paved trench was enlarged and extended into the main streets of Rome. The top was enclosed by a barrel vault, with openings in the street allowing the rainwater to drain into the sewer. This was eventually named the Cloaca Maxima. Public toilets were connected to the sewer carrying waste out of Rome into the Tiber River. The Cloaca Maxima has been enlarged and repaired over the years and serves Rome to this day.

GOOD WATER FOR ALL

Clean water flowing in from the 1,300 miles (2,100 km) of aqueducts provided a daily average of 130 gallons (490 liters) of fresh spring water per Roman citizen. The abundance of water gave Roman builders a new idea—public baths. These were originally large pools for public bathing. But as they became social centers, other features such as steam baths, exercise rooms, game rooms, gardens, and libraries were added. We might call such a place a health club today. And it was free. By 100 A.D. there were several hundred baths in Rome. One of the largest, built in 212 A.D., was the Baths of Caracalla, which covered 27 acres (11 ha) and was so large that 1,600 people could bathe at the same time.

Roman baths in Bath, England

HEALTH RULES ARE MADE

As medical science progressed, the leaders of Rome began to see a need for standardizing medical care to protect the health of the people. Physicians were required to have a good education and to have a license. Inspectors strolled through markets confiscating and destroying the spoiled food. Other inspectors checked on the purity of the aqueduct water and on the proper functioning of the sewers and baths.

To avoid the spread of disease from the dead to the living, laws forbade the burial of the dead within the city. Those with diseases thought to be highly contagious, such as leprosy, were kept in isolated areas.

MEDICAL CARE FOR ALL

Ever the organizers, the Romans provided health care for a variety of people. Soldiers and sailors had their own doctors. The poor could seek medical care through the public medical care service. A center where doctors could focus their efforts on caring for the sick—a hospital—was built. The Roman hospital design was similar to that used today, with wards, dining rooms for the staff, kitchens, and apothecaries (pharmacies). The public hospital is considered Rome's greatest contribution to medicine.

Still, much was not known about protecting health. For a thousand years Rome had loomed as a giant over the world. But as the fifth century dawned, the Romans seemed to lose their zest for building, growing, and organizing. Some think this may have been caused by malaria. The Romans, with their primitive pumps and digging equipment, never really conquered the marshes. (Modern scientists and engineers have learned that draining the marshes is next to impossible and that adding oil to the marsh water keeps the mosquitoes from breeding.) Another theory for the decline of

Rome holds that the lead in the aqueduct piping gradually gave the people lead poisoning.

It is ironic to think that the very people who pioneered public health may have died out because they failed to identify and solve these public health problems.

8

THE ROMANS' WORLD: CALENDARS AND MAPS

Among the treasures that victorious Roman legions brought back from the conquered Greek town of Cantania, on the island of Sicily, was a sundial. It was installed in the Forum in the center of Rome in 263 B.C. For one hundred years Romans passed it every day, never realizing that it gave the wrong time, never thinking that a sundial built to serve a town 330 miles (530 km) southeast of Rome could not accurately measure the day in Rome.

By 164 B.C., Romans studying Greek writings learned that the sundial's pointer should be matched to the position of the sun in the sky at Rome's latitude. The pointer, or **gnomon**, is supposed to point north and be parallel to the earth's axis. In those days, sundials were built for specific locations, with the gnomon parallel to the earth's axis at that site. Today we can use a compass to quickly determine north and adjust our gnomon accordingly.

Few Romans were interested in astronomy. They did not concern themselves with questions like "what is earth's place in the universe?" or "how do the planets move?" Rather they looked for the practical uses of astronomy.

MAKING A BETTER CALENDAR

For centuries people had struggled with a lunar calendar, using the new moon as the first day of the new month and producing a 355-day year. But people's lives are governed more by the seasons, which are determined by the position of the sun relative to that of the earth. The lunar calendar wasn't much use to the farmer, for example. The farmer needed to know when to plant and how to make the best use of the spring and summer and was forced to use the position of the stars to plan the planting schedule.

In 46 B.C. when the day for the spring festival, Floralia, came in the middle of summer, the Roman emperor Julius Caesar decided something had to be done. He consulted the Greek astronomer, Sosigenes, who advised that a 365-day year be established. An extra day every four years, producing leap year, would even the years out. This is the Julian calendar.

The months of the Julian calendar were named Januarius, for the Roman god Janus; Februarius, because it was the month of purification, making amends for wrongs; Martius, for the Roman god Mars; April, May, and June for the Latin words for opening, growth, and ripening, to signify the growing season; Julius, to honor Julius Caesar; Augustus, for Caesar Augustus, who succeeded Julius Caesar as emperor; September, October, November, and December, which were the seventh, eighth, ninth, and tenth months in the old calendar.

Although the Julian calendar was set up to have 365¼ days, the actual average length of the Julian calendar year was 365 days and a small fraction, 11 minutes and 14 seconds. This fraction added up to one day every 128 years. In one thousand years, the calendar lost eight days.

Pope Gregory XIII reformed the Julian calendar in 1582. First he ordered that the next day after October 5, 1582, should be October 15, 1582. That made up for the lost days. Then he added other small adjustments, which produced the calendar we use today.

JULIUS CAESAR'S FARMER'S ALMANAC

The Julian calendar gave the Roman farmer a calendar to plant by. To this Julius Caesar added a kind of farmer's almanac, *De Astris*, about the stars. In it Caesar, who knew a great deal about the stars, provided information that used the position of stars and other heavenly bodies to predict the advance and nature of the seasons.

As a general, conqueror, and explorer, Julius Caesar had a natural interest in geography. His commentaries on the Gallic Wars, written during his conquest of Gaul (what is today France, Belgium, and part of the Netherlands), provide descriptions of many of the places he visited. Since he had few, if any, useful maps, Caesar questioned many local inhabitants during his march north. He kept notes on their responses, giving us an enduring record of the manners and customs of the people. His notes described rivers, mountains, and forests.

Julius Caesar explored Britain, describing it as a triangular island and estimating its size. He visited Hibernia (Ireland), describing it as half as big as Britain and to the west. He was the first to discover the Isle of Man, off the British coast.

THE GEOGRAPHY OF ROME

Julius Caesar's commentaries on the Gallic Wars, along with notes written by other Roman generals, were used by the great Greek geographer Strabo (STRAY bo). He wrote the seventeen-volume *Geography*, in which he provided a general description of earth's

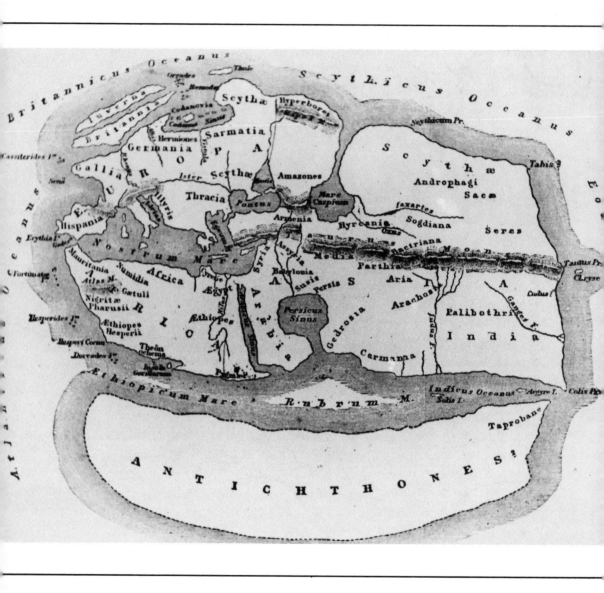

Roman map from the
first century A.D.

features, its rivers, mountains, deserts, and oceans. Further, Strabo described the differences between parts of the earth and how people lived in those different regions. Although Strabo traveled a great deal to collect his information, he credited the Romans for writings and notes that gave him a picture of certain parts of the world he could never have gained on his own.

In 44 B.C., Julius Caesar used his authority as emperor of Rome to order a survey and mapping of the entire Roman empire. The assignment fell to Marcus Vispanius Agrippa—master engineer, builder of aqueducts, roads, sewers, and marvels such as the Pantheon. Somehow the Romans had managed to conquer and rule most of the world without such a map. Now they would have one. But Caesar would not live to see it. He was murdered by his political enemies in March of 44 B.C.

Agrippa had at his disposal the instruments and techniques he used for building. He also had measurements of the length of many Roman roads. But still there was much to be done to map and chart the way those roads fit together and what the lay of the land was like around them. The map had to show where rivers crossed and where valleys and mountains were and how far they were from each other.

It took Agrippa nearly thirty years to finish his project. The final map was so big that a special building was constructed to house it.

9

THE ROMAN LEGACY

The year was 27 B.C., the first year of Pax Romana. Rome was at peace with most of the world for the years between 27 B.C. and 162 A.D. There was little need for Roman legions to march forth to invade or defend. Instead, Roman soldiers drew assignments to work on building projects. Magnificent cities with splendid graceful structures and modern water and sanitation systems offered a life-style to the Roman Empire that would not be seen again in history for hundreds of years. It was the golden age for Rome.

In 162 A.D. invaders began hammering at the eastern and northern borders of the empire, and Pax Romana was shattered. By 180 A.D. the "age of gold had turned to rust and iron," as one Roman historian observed. Although the empire would endure for another three hundred years, a decline in technological progress was a part of that rust in 180 A.D.

WHY DID THIS HAPPEN?

Certainly there were social problems lurking beneath the glittering surface of Pax Romana. For years slave labor had been used to perform many of the back-breaking tasks needed to build the beautiful domes and graceful arched bridges. The slaves were sometimes prisoners of war taken in battle, but two hundred years of peace had severely reduced Rome's labor force.

In addition to slave labor, Romans were running out of natural resources by the end of the second century. They needed coal, iron, wood, and water to continue their phenomenal technological achievements.

The answer to Rome's lagging decline in technological progress may well lie in the Roman's fundamental lack of interest in science. Most Romans lived their lives by a belief, or set of rules, called Stoicism. Stoicism called for correct conduct and duty and for living one's life in a very useful, practical way. All knowledge not of practical use was rejected.

The Romans saw science as a way to improve architecture, medicine, and engineering. The Roman observed nature but did not care for biology. The Roman was a good engineer but made no contributions to mathematics. Romans revised the calendar but added nothing to the knowledge of astronomy.

Thus, the Romans took from science but gave nothing back. Gradually, the stream of scientific ideas that could be used for technological ideas dried up.

Technology and science often work together. Even here, the Romans failed the growth of science by failing to invent the kinds of devices and instruments that could have helped scientists. For example, microscopes and telescopes could have been built, since it is known that the Romans understood a great deal about optics.

In fact, Roman glassmakers invented the first magnifying glass—a small bottle of water. The simple lens worked on the principle that light bends as it passes through different materials and makes images larger. Seneca, a Roman philosopher and statesman (3 B.C. to 65 A.D.), wrote: "Letters, however small and dim, are comparatively large and distinct when seen through a glass globe filled with water." But apparently, a magnifying lens seemed of little practical use to the Romans. That magnification might serve a scientific purpose—to learn more about living organisms and the stars—did not occur to the Romans.

As scientific ideas waned, the Romans looked for magic effects in science. From their interest in astronomy as a way to measure the year, they turned to astrology, which used the position of the stars to predict events. Their talent for chemistry, stimulated by their success in metal refining, was overcome by their interest in alchemy, whose practitioners often sought magical ways to change lead into gold. Those interested in plants turned their talents to devising often ridiculous potions for treating the sick.

THE DARK AGES

The year 476, when Rome was finally defeated by the German tribes to the north, signaled the end of the ancient world and the beginning of the Dark Ages. For nearly one thousand years Europe made little intellectual or technical progress. The beautiful domed buildings and arches, the roads, and the aqueducts fell into ruins. People went back to living in thatched huts and bathing in the river.

As the dark shadows fell on scientific inquiry, some Roman historians began to collect and describe the science of ancient Greece and Rome. Martianus Capella, who lived in the fifth century A.D., compiled a history of geometry, geography, astronomy, and mathematics. Boethius and Cassiodorus, other fifth-century writers, provided copies and summaries of the work of great Greek scientists such as Euclid, the mathematician, and Ptolemy, the astronomer. These writings survived the Dark Ages and waited for the later scientist to find inspiration in them. Out of these ancient ideas, the Renaissance period came to be. The word **renaissance** means "rebirth."

The Renaissance began in fourteenth-century Florence in the very area where the Etruscans once flourished. The intellectual and artistic movement grew and spread throughout Europe.

A SECOND CHANCE
FOR ROMAN MEDICINE

A number of the medical treatments used today have their origins in the writings of Roman medical scientists, many of whom were actually Greeks. One of the first ancient medical books to emerge in Florence was written by Celsus, who described the Roman physician Asclepiades' theory that there were ways to treat disease, that one need not rely entirely on the body healing itself.

Galen's *The Uses of the Parts of the Body of Man* served as a basic anatomy book until well into the sixteenth century. Unfortunately, some of his incorrect theories, accepted because they were those of the respected and famous Galen, held back the progress of medicine until recent times.

Apollonius' *Commentary*, which describes the treatment of bone dislocations and provides helpful drawings, was used by physicians until well after the Renaissance.

Rufus' books on anatomy and disease proved an inspiration to Arab physicians in the Middle Ages and to those who followed.

Soranus' *On Diseases of Women* served as a guide for midwives during the sixth century. The book was rediscovered by nineteenth-century physicians.

OTHER ROMAN IDEAS
LEFT TO THE WORLD

Engineers would turn to the writings of the Roman aqueduct designer Frontinus for guidance in building a water supply system. As late as 1850 Paris was still using his measuring system. In 1842, when a British commission was appointed to investigate ways to

improve the health of London's people, they used the Roman sanitation system as one of their guidelines. London had nothing like it.

Romans are credited with developing many of the public health ideas we use today—gymnasiums, food inspection, military hospitals, medical insurance, medical schools, and the licensing of physicians.

Many devices and structures are in use today thanks to the inventiveness of the Romans. Roman engineers perfected bridges, sewers, staircases, roads, seaports, surveying, orchard planting, and oyster cultivation. They invented the glass windowpane, the milestone, scales with weights for weighing things, chemical fertilizer, the theater curtain, stenography, and many tools—scissors, the plane, the punch, the borer, the brace and bit, the door key, and the bellows with a nozzle.

Perhaps the greatest contribution that Rome made to the world was its architecture. The traveler to Rome can tour the Pantheon and tread the cobblestones of the ruins of the Colosseum and realize that Roman architecture changed the look of cities forever.

The Pantheon, in Rome
(exterior and interior)

GLOSSARY

Alloy—A mixture of two or more metals or a metal and a nonmetal. See Brass and Bronze.

Aqueducts—Channels for carrying water; in Roman times they were concrete-walled and supported by tall arches.

Barrel vault—A long, thick concrete arch in the shape of half a barrel.

Brass—An alloy of copper and zinc.

Bronze—An alloy of copper and tin and sometimes other metals.

Concrete—A mixture of powdered lime and water to which sand and stone are added.

Cross vaults—(groined): Crossing of two long, thick arches at right angles to produce a large square-roofed building.

Gnomon—The pointer on a sundial; the position or length of its shadow indicates the time of day.

Hypocaustum—An underground home heating system developed by the Romans.

Insulae—Roman apartment buildings having more than one story.

Malaria—A disease characterized by periods of chills and fever, transmitted by the bite of a certain kind of mosquito.

Renaissance—Literally, rebirth; a period from the fourteenth to the seventeenth century in Europe marked by the flowering of art and literature and the beginning of modern science.

Science—Knowledge obtained through study, practice, and testing.

Villas—Country houses having more than one wing.

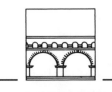

FOR FURTHER READING

Bailey, Cyril, ed. *The Legacy of Rome*. New York: Oxford University Press, 1962.

Boorstin, Daniel J. *The Discoverers*. New York: Random House, 1983.

Cary, M., and Scullard, H. H. *A History of Rome*. New York: St. Martin's Press, 1977.

Casson, Lionel. *Daily Life in Ancient Rome*. New York: McGraw-Hill, 1975.

Clark, Ronald W. *Works of Man*. New York: Viking, 1985.

Cunlife, Barry. *Rome and Her Empire*. New York: McGraw-Hill, 1978.

DeCamp, L. Sprague. *The Ancient Engineers*. New York: Doubleday, 1963.

Grimal, Pierre. *The Civilization of Rome*. New York: Simon and Schuster, 1963.

Hadas, Moses. *Imperial Rome*. New York: Time/Life, 1965.

Hamblin, Dora Jane. *The Etruscans*. New York: Time/Life, 1975.

Hill, Donald. *A History of Engineering in Classical and Medieval Times*. La Salle, Ill.: Open Court, 1984.

Hoyt, Edwin P. *A Short History of Science*. New York: John Day, 1965.

Landels, J. G. *Engineering in the Ancient World*. Berkeley and Los Angeles: University of California Press, 1978.

Mills, Dorothy. *The Book of the Ancient Romans*. New York: Putnam's, 1937.

Ronan, Colin A. *Science: Its History and Development*. New York: Facts on File, 1982.

Singer, Charles, and Underwood, E. Ashworth. *A Short History of Medicine*. New York: Oxford University Press, 1962.

Starr, Chester G. *A History of the Ancient World*. New York: Oxford University Press, 1983.

Taton, Rene. *Ancient and Medieval Science*. New York: Basic, 1963.

Thorwald, Jurgen. *Science and Secrets of Early Medicine*. London: Thames & Hudson, 1962.

INDEX